Artists' Workshop

Portraits

Penny King and Clare Roundhill

A & C Black · London

Designed by Jane Warring

Illustrations by Lindy Norton

Children's pictures and sculptures by
Amber Civardi, Davina Clarke, Camilla Cramsie,
Charlotte Downham, Ellie Grace, Lara Haworth, Lucinda Howells,
Sophie Johns, Abby Kirvan, Rosanna Kirvan, Freddie Marriage,
Gussie Pownhall, Leo Thomson, Lucy Stratton, Isabella Milne,
Victoria Arbuthnot, Leonora Bowen

Photographs by Peter Millard

Reprinted 1999, 2002
First paperback edition 1996
First published 1996 in hardback by
A & C Black Publishers Ltd
37 Soho Square, London, W1D 3QZ
www.acblack.com

Created by
Thumbprint Books

ISBN 0-7136-6700-1

Printed and bound in Singapore

A & C Black uses paper produced with elemental chlorine-free pulp,
harvested from managed, sustainable forests.

Cover photograph: Vincent Van Gogh Postman Roulin, 1889
When Van Gogh lived in the South of France, he became friends with this postman,
who brought him letters from his brother Theo. Van Gogh painted several portraits of him

Contents

4   Looking at portraits

6   Egyptian effects

8   An imaginary journey

10   Magnificent mosaics

12   Making a mosaic picture

14   Swirls of colour

16   Painting a self-portrait

18   Line and pattern portraits

20   Line design

22   Skinny sculptures

24   Wiry walkers

26   Photo portraits

28   Photo-fitting

30   More about the artists

31   Other things to do

32   Index

Looking at portraits

'Every time I paint a portrait, I lose a friend', a famous American artist, called John Singer Sargent, once said. That's probably because he managed to show the likeness of the people he painted too truthfully.

Before photography was invented, important people, such as kings, queens or rich merchants, paid artists to paint their portraits.

These portraits not only showed what people looked like, they were also full of clues about their lives. Rulers were often shown with their crowns and robes. Rich people were shown wearing expensive clothes and jewels. Soldiers wore their uniforms and carried weapons.

The invention of photography gave people a much easier way to make realistic portraits. Artists thought there was no point in copying photography, and started thinking of new ways to create portraits. They often used colour in different and unusual ways, to express a person's feelings and moods.

François-Hubert Drouais (1727-1775)
Madame de Pompadour Musée Condé, Chantilly

Portraits can be created in many ways - as paintings, drawings, photographs or sculptures. This book contains six portraits, two very old and the rest more modern. Each of them has been created using a different technique.

You can learn what gave the artists the ideas for creating these portraits, and discover how they made them. Borrow their ideas, mix them with your ideas and create portraits of your own. The pictures done by children will help you.

You can create a portrait any way you choose. Either make it look as much as possible like the person you are painting, or give an impression of the person's mood. You can show a front view or a side view (known as a profile).

Your portrait might be in full colour or in black and white. You can make your subject look pretty or ugly and frightening - or you can paint a portrait of yourself. This is called a self-portrait. The choice is up to you!

Egyptian effects

Would you believe that this picture is over 3,000 years old? It was painted on the floor of the tomb of an Ancient Egyptian official. It is a portrait of a king, called Amenophis I, surrounded by symbols - pictures with special meanings.

Dead King Amenophis I © British Museum

The Egyptians believed that when people died, they went to a new world with their belongings. They looked forward to their new life and were not frightened of dying.

Their bodies were dried out and wrapped in linen bandages. These preserved bodies were called mummies. The mummies were put in coffins inside painted tombs.

Every picture around the portrait of Amenophis I has an important meaning.

▶ The sun is shown as a red disc moving across the sky on wings. It is protected by two serpents.

◀ The cobra on the king's forehead is a symbol of the sun. It spits fire at the king's enemies to protect him from them.

▶ The feather pattern on the king's clothes shows that he was mummified. The pattern represents the wings of the goddesses wrapped around his body to protect him.

crook

flail

◀ The ankh is a symbol of everlasting life. Only kings and queens were allowed to carry one, since only they had the power to give or take a life.

▲ Kings are often shown carrying a crook and a flail in their hands. These are symbols of kingship.

▼ The vulture represents Upper Egypt, which this king once ruled.

▲ The falcon is the symbol of the sun god, Horus.

▲ The eye represents the eye of Horus. It was damaged during a fight for the throne of Egypt, and restored by magic. It shows that everything is still perfect and healthy even after death.

An imaginary journey

Imagine you or a friend are moving to a new world. Decide what you would take with you on your journey and then paint a portrait surrounded by these important possessions.

Perhaps you would take a favourite pet, toy, book, hat, or the food you like best. Paint pictures which show your interests, just like the Egyptians did.

Pastel portrait

Use a brown pastel to draw a friend's profile on a big piece of white paper. Include her neck, shoulders and part of her body. Look at the colours on the Egyptian tomb painting. Choose similar colours for your portrait.

You can mix pastels together to make different colours. Press hard and use lots of strokes to get a dark colour. Rub them gently into the paper with your fingertips or cotton wool.

Draw a pattern all over the clothes and colour it in with pastels. Make the background a pale, sandy colour. Draw pictures of your friend's favourite things all over it.

Egyptian mummy portrait

Ask your mummy to sit sideways between a lamp and some paper stuck to the wall behind her. Draw carefully around her shadow.

Paint her face with watercolours or poster paint, trying as hard as you can to match her skin, hair and eye colours. To give her an Egyptian look, outline her eyes and the whole portrait in black.

When it is dry, cut out the picture and glue it to a big piece of brightly coloured paper. Ask your mummy what things she would take to a new world and then paint them on the background paper.

If you need to add any details, let the bottom colours dry first otherwise the paints might run into each other. Give each picture a dark outline.

Your favourite things

Put on the things you would like to wear on an imaginary journey to a new world - perhaps a favourite hat or cap. Look at yourself in the mirror and paint your portrait on a sheet of brightly coloured paper. Outline all the features with black paint.

Choose ten important things you would take with you. Cut out pictures of them from magazines, and glue them around your portrait.

Magnificent mosaics

This picture is called a mosaic. Mosaics are made with lots of small pieces of a hard material, such as stone, tile or glass. The pieces are glued or cemented close together on a flat surface.

Head of Neptune, Roman Ancient Art & Architecture Collection, London

This mosaic shows the head of Neptune, the Roman god of the sea. The Romans believed he lived in an underwater palace with his wife.

He is always shown as an old man with long wavy hair and a long spiky beard. Sometimes, he holds a three-pronged spear called a trident.

▶ Long ago, the Greeks and Romans used mosaics to decorate their floors and walls. These often told stories of people, animals or battles.

◀ Sometimes, as a joke, the mosaic makers put in pictures of fish bones and other scraps of food, so that it looked as if people had dropped them on the floor.

▼ Look how the main shapes of the mosaic have a dark outline. Mosaics were meant to be seen at a distance. The outlines helped them to stand out.

▲ Other people, called Byzantines, made magnificent glass and gold mosaics of emperors and saints dressed in rich-looking costumes.

Making a mosaic picture

Make your own mosaic pictures using pieces cut from magazines or wrapping paper. You might prefer to print a mosaic picture instead.

Magazine mosaic

Before you begin your mosaic picture, make a coloured sketch of it first.

Look through old magazines for the colours you need. Choose colours that match the sketch you have drawn.

Cut out big squares for the background and small squares for the details of the face and clothes. You may need more of some colours than others.

Cut lots of shades of the same colour - some dark, some light. Keep each shade in a separate pile.

Glue the squares on another piece of paper, matching the colours of your sketch. It takes quite a long time, but it's worth it!

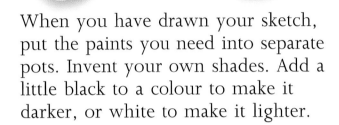

Printed mosaic

Cut an old sponge into cubes - some big, some small.

When you have drawn your sketch, put the paints you need into separate pots. Invent your own shades. Add a little black to a colour to make it darker, or white to make it lighter.

Before you start your real picture, practise printing on newspaper first. Use one sponge cube for each shade. Print the eyes, nose and mouth first. Then fill in the rest of the face.

Wrapping paper mosaic

Cut coloured paper, wrapping paper, or old birthday and Christmas cards into squares. Use them to create different textures and patterns in your picture.

13

Swirls of colour

Vincent Van Gogh, a Dutch artist, painted this portrait of himself a few months before he died. He was one of the first painters to use colours to show his moods and feelings, instead of trying to paint things in realistic colours. How do you think he was feeling when he painted this picture?

Vincent Van Gogh Self-Portrait 1889. Musée d'Orsay, Paris

Van Gogh painted very fast. He used thick, bold strokes that swirl, curl and spiral. Sometimes he was in such a hurry, he squeezed paint straight on to a canvas and spread it with his fingers.

Colour was very important to Van Gogh. His early pictures of Dutch peasants were dark and sad, to show what hard lives these people led.

Later, he moved to the South of France and started painting with purer, brighter colours, which showed the shimmering heat and light of his surroundings. Van Gogh loved nature and liked painting out of doors. His pictures of flowers and trees are full of joy and yellow sunshine.

But Van Gogh himself was often unhappy. Once, when he was very miserable, he cut off part of his ear. He painted several self-portraits after that which show his loneliness. The pale, icy colours of the self-portrait opposite emphasise his unhappy and lonely feelings.

Painting a self-portrait

Use the same rich style as Van Gogh to paint a self-portrait that shows how you feel as well as how you look. The best ways to get a good likeness of yourself are to copy a photograph or to look at your face in the mirror as you draw. Use thick paint, made of PVA glue or flour mixed with poster paint.

Drawing faces

Draw an oval face. Lightly sketch a line across it, half way down. This is the position for your eyes and tops of your ears. Draw another line half way between this line and the chin. The tip of your nose will rest here. Halve the bottom section to find where to draw your mouth.

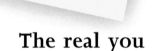

The real you

Do you have a big or small nose, brown or blue eyes, fair or dark hair? Paint a portrait that looks as much like you as possible, mixing colours to match your features. To get rough and smooth textures, spread on swirls, dots, lines and dashes of thick paint with a brush, lolly stick or even your fingertips.

A moody portrait

How are you feeling today - hot with anger, pale with tiredness, or sparkling with excitement? Once you've decided, paint a portrait of yourself using colours that match your mood. Don't worry about making your skin colour realistic. Just use the colours that you think show your feelings best.

Background blast

Paint a portrait of yourself, but this time give it a moody background to show how you feel. It might have swirls of yellow and orange if you are in a happy mood, blue if you are feeling sad, purple and black if you are angry, or sparks and dashes of red if you are excited.

Line and pattern portraits

The famous Spanish artist, Pablo Picasso, created this portrait using lines and patterns to give it texture and a feeling of depth. He coloured only the areas that he thought were the most important.

Pablo Picasso *Dora Maar Seated in a Wicker Chair,* 1938. Metropolitan Museum of Art, Jacques and Natasha Gelman Collection, New York

Picasso met Dora Maar, the woman in the picture, in a cafe in Paris. He was fascinated by her hands with their long red fingernails.

He watched Dora play a curious game with a knife. She flicked the blade between her fingers, sometimes cutting herself.

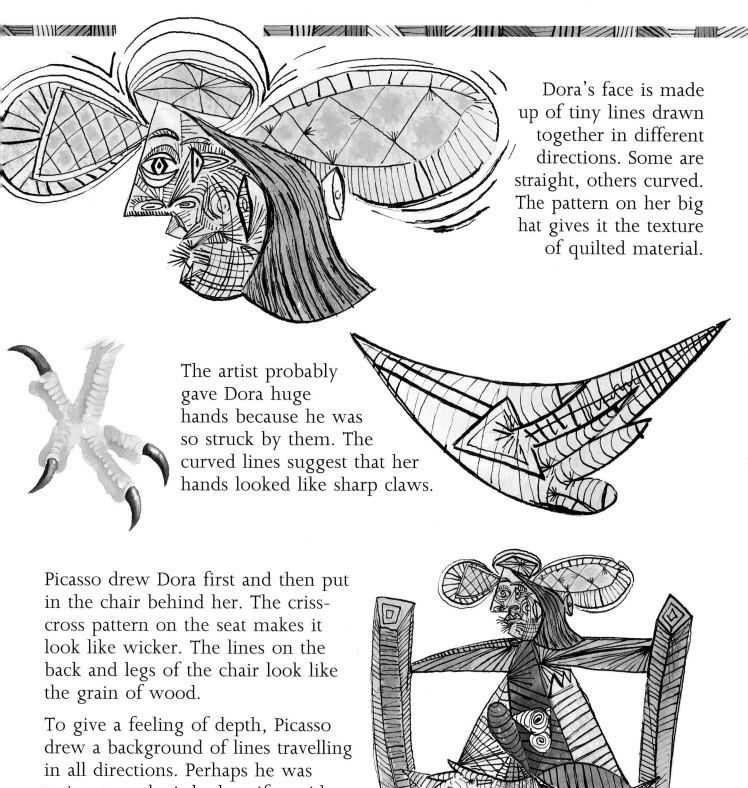

Dora's face is made up of tiny lines drawn together in different directions. Some are straight, others curved. The pattern on her big hat gives it the texture of quilted material.

The artist probably gave Dora huge hands because he was so struck by them. The curved lines suggest that her hands looked like sharp claws.

Picasso drew Dora first and then put in the chair behind her. The criss-cross pattern on the seat makes it look like wicker. The lines on the back and legs of the chair look like the grain of wood.

To give a feeling of depth, Picasso drew a background of lines travelling in all directions. Perhaps he was trying to make it look as if a spider was spinning its web around Dora, protecting her and trapping her at the same time.

Dora looks a little like a doll sitting in a toy chair, her eyes staring and arms loosely folded. There is something about her that doesn't seem quite real.

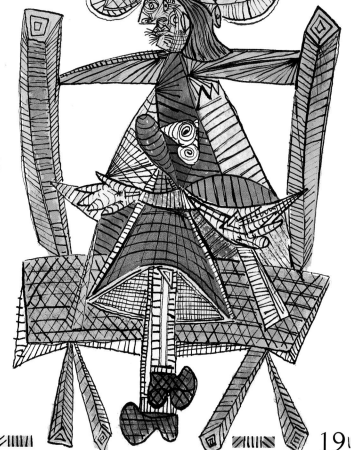

Line design

Have a go at drawing your own line and pattern portraits. The lines can be thick or thin, curved or wavy, close together or far apart, straight or crooked, zig-zagged or criss-crossed. Use the lines to create different textures - perhaps a woollen jersey, a cotton dress, thick hair or smooth skin.

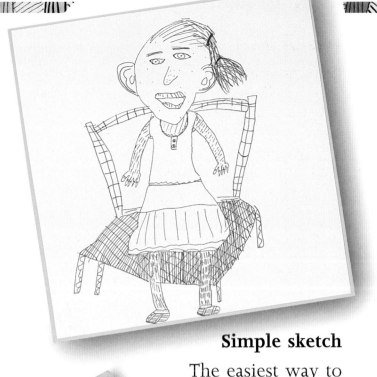

Simple sketch

The easiest way to draw someone sitting in a chair is to draw the person first and then put in the chair behind her.

Funny face

Draw the outline of a friend's head in profile. Decide which is her strongest feature, perhaps her nose, and draw it a bit bigger than you normally would.

Draw in the hair, eyes, ears and mouth. They don't have to be true to life. Look at how Picasso has muddled up Dora's features and given her bell-shaped ears, big flaring nostrils and strange-looking eyes.

Fill in the face with tiny lines, either straight or curved. Use crayons or felt-tip pens to colour the parts you think are the most important.

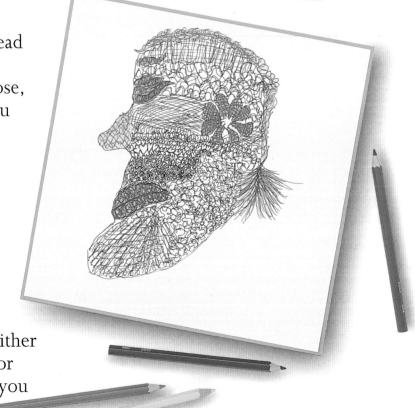

Lots of lines

Draw a portrait of a friend sitting in a chair, making it look as much like Picasso's picture as you can.

Fill in the face, hair, clothes, shoes and chair with different kinds of lines and patterns. Use the lines to give your picture texture and a feeling of depth. Paint the most important parts.

Criss-crossed, waxy portrait

This time draw the outline of your portrait using a felt-tip pen. Fill it in with lines and patterns, using a coloured wax crayon. Add a web of lines in the background.

Use different coloured felt-tip pens to colour over the most important areas of your picture. The wax lines resist the felt-tip pens to give a very unusual effect.

Skinny sculptures

A Swiss artist, called Alberto
Giacometti, made this sculpture out
of bronze. He called it Man Pointing.
Giacometti is well-known for his
long, thin sculptures of people.
As he worked at his sculptures, they
became thinner and thinner.

Alberto Giacometti Man Pointing, 1947 Tate Gallery, London

Giacometti was influenced by a group of artists, called Surrealists. They preferred to paint pictures from their imagination, from memory or from dreams rather than from real life.

This sketch and the painting below were inspired, but not drawn, by Giacometti.

Alberto Giacometti Three Men Walking I 1948, Courtesy of Association Alberto and Annette Giacometti, Paris

The people in Giacometti's sculptures and paintings often look sad and lonely. He thought they looked more lifelike if they were very small or very thin.

He liked to use earthy colours in his paintings and sculptures. His favourite colour was grey. Even though people told him to use bright colours, he took no notice.

Wiry walkers

Create your own Giacometti-style
sculptures using wire, tin foil, clay
or papier mâché. Ask friends to
pose for you outside in the
afternoon sun. Look at and sketch
the long, thin shadows their
bodies make. Draw all sorts of
different poses to give you ideas
for your skinny sculptures.

◀ Wire man

Bend a very long piece of thick,
plastic-coated garden wire in half.
Make a loop at the top for the head.
Twist the wires together to make a
neck. Bend and twist each wire to
make arms. Then twist the wires
together for the body. Finally, bend
up the wires and twist them
together to make legs. Bend
the figure into one of the
poses you have
sketched.

◀ Tin foil figure

Make a wire figure as you did before. Cover it with strips of tin foil, squashed firmly around the body. To make your sculpture look more colourful, you can add shiny sweet papers. Press it into modelling clay if you want your figure to stand up.

▼ Clay child

Make a wire figure. Roll balls of self-hardening clay into soft, sticky sausage shapes. Pull off small bits at a time and press them on to the wire frame. If you want, you could paint colourful decorations all over your clay figure when it has dried.

▲ Papier mâché person

Mix half a cup of flour with enough water to make a thick, smooth paste. Add a tablespoon of PVA glue. Dip strips of coloured magazine pages into the mixture. Wrap them around a wire figure. Try not to get too much glue mixture on to the paper strips.

Photo portraits

Can you see how this portrait is made from lots of photographs of the same person, taken from different angles? This technique is called photo-montage. The portrait is by a British artist, called David Hockney. It shows his mother.

David Hockney Mother Yorkshire Moors 1982 © D. Hockney 1982

Hockney wanted to show every detail of his mother. He took photos of her from both the front and the sides.

Then he joined them together in his picture. Some pictures were taken closer up than others. Which ones?

Notice how the photos overlap to bring out particular features, such as hair and wrinkles. They are carefully arranged and pasted down to make a whole portrait. Hockney didn't worry that the edges were ragged.

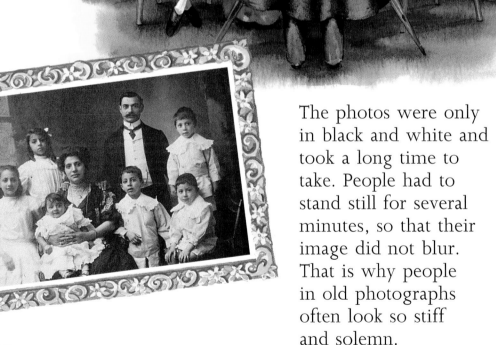

The first cameras were big and heavy. Only a few people knew how to use them. Photographers had studios where families went to have their pictures taken. They stood or sat in front of a painted cloth background.

The photos were only in black and white and took a long time to take. People had to stand still for several minutes, so that their image did not blur. That is why people in old photographs often look so stiff and solemn.

Modern cameras are cheaper and easier to use. Anyone can buy a camera and take quick photographs in colour. Compare a photo of yourself with one of your granny when she was little.

Photo-fitting

Here's a chance to create your own montages using photographs, drawings or pictures cut from magazines. They'll look even better if you use side views as well as front views.

Spend time laying down the pictures in different positions until you are pleased with the way your montage looks. You can either overlap the pictures or leave gaps to give really interesting shapes.

Photo montage

Ask someone to take lots of photographs of you while you are outside facing the sun. Get the person to take pictures of different features of your face - your forehead, eyes, chin, ears, hair, neck, mouth and nose, both side view and front view.

The photographer will have to move around you, but you must keep very still. Remind him to keep the camera as still as possible while he shoots.

When the photographs have been developed, choose the ones you think will look best for your montage. Cut them up if you need to, and then lay them out to give an interesting image.

Glue the photographs on to stiff card, two at a time, so that you don't disturb the whole picture. Glue the bottom ones first.

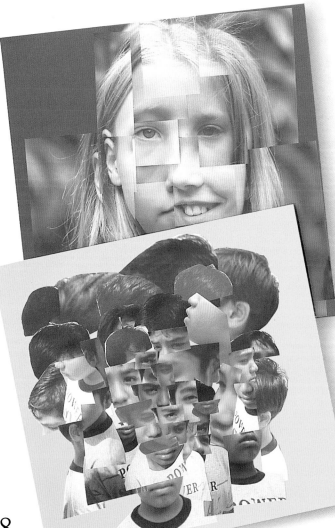

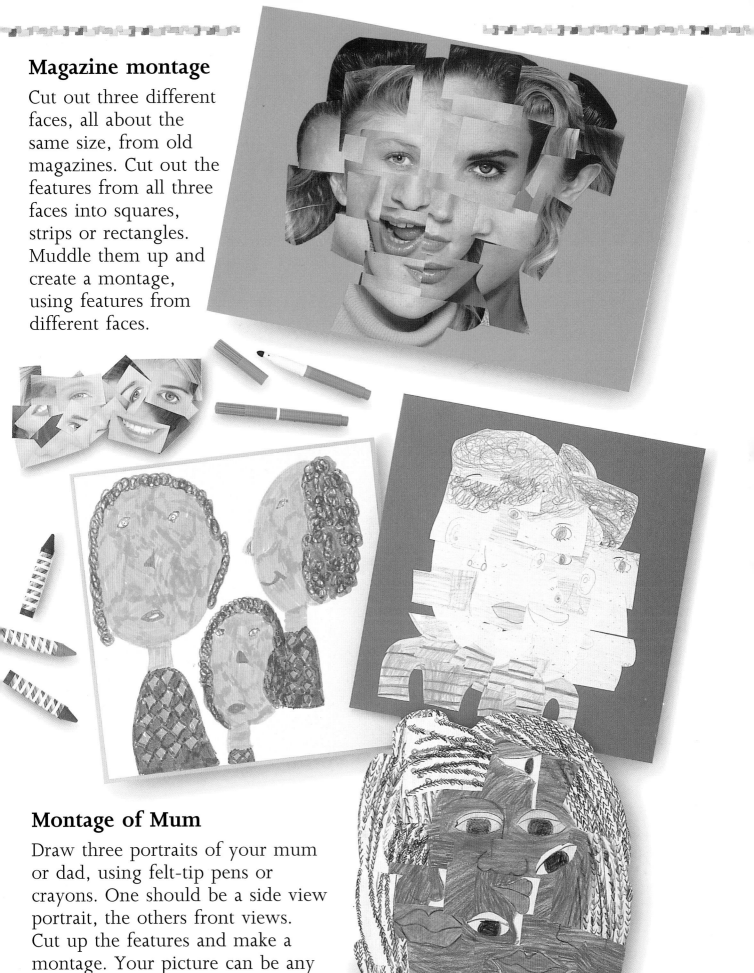

Magazine montage

Cut out three different faces, all about the same size, from old magazines. Cut out the features from all three faces into squares, strips or rectangles. Muddle them up and create a montage, using features from different faces.

Montage of Mum

Draw three portraits of your mum or dad, using felt-tip pens or crayons. One should be a side view portrait, the others front views. Cut up the features and make a montage. Your picture can be any shape you like.

More about the artists

Egyptian painters

Dead King Amenophis I, 1050 BC

Egyptian artists were especially trained to paint spells on coffins, and scenes on the walls of tombs of kings and other important people. People believed that the spells would protect the dead, and that the scenes would work by magic to give them everything they needed for living in the next world. The artists ground their own colours from minerals and used charcoal for black and ochre for red.

Roman mosaic makers
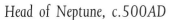

Head of Neptune, c.500AD

Mosaic makers were very skilled. They made their own cubes, called tesserae, from different coloured materials, such as sandstone, limestone, marble and brick. First they sawed the hard stone into thin sticks. Then they hammered these sticks over a sharp chisel head to cut them into cubes. Mosaics are very hard-wearing. Many of them still survive today, many years after they were first made.

Vincent Van Gogh

(1853- 1890   Dutch)
Self-Portrait, 1889

Van Gogh worked as a schoolmaster and a missionary before he became a painter. He taught himself to draw and to paint with oil paints. He painted everyday scenes, such as landscapes, flowers, his bedroom, a chair and portraits of himself and his neighbours, in a bold and exciting way. He sold only one painting during his lifetime, but now his paintings sell for millions of pounds. Perhaps his most famous paintings are of sunflowers. Van Gogh signed his paintings with just his first name, Vincent.

Pablo Picasso

(1881 - 1973   Spanish)
Dora Maar seated in a Wicker Chair, 1938

Picasso was one of the most important and famous artists of this century. His father was an artist as well, and taught him to draw when he was a young child. Picasso spent his life experimenting with new ways of painting and sculpting. He helped to invent a style of art called Cubism, which showed objects, landscapes and people in geometric shapes, often in browns or greys.

Alberto Giacometti

(1901 - 1966   Swiss)
Man Pointing, 1947

By the time Giacometti was a teenager, he was already good at sculpture and painting. Later, he made sculptures of thin human figures, either on their own or in groups. These were usually set upon thick heavy bases. Giacometti was interested in the shapes a figure made in the space around it, and in the relationship between several figures. *Man Pointing* is one of his most famous sculptures. His paintings were almost always of people, painted in shades of brown and grey.

David Hockney

(Born 1937   British)
Mother photo-montage, 1982

David Hockney is a popular modern painter. Many of his paintings show the people he knows or the places where he has lived. He has spent many years in California, USA, and has painted all sorts of views of it. One of his most famous paintings is *A Bigger Splash* (1967), which shows a Californian swimming pool. He often uses photography and has created all sorts of photo-montages.

Other things to do

1 Make a collection of portraits. See how many different types you can find - for example, coins, stamps, photographs, drawings, cartoons and postcards. They will give you ideas for creating portraits of your own.

3 Find a big sheet of clear plastic and a passport-sized photograph of yourself. Draw a dozen or more outlines of your face on the plastic, using the photo as a guide. Now draw all sorts of different hairstyles on the plastic - long, short, curly and even multi-coloured. Put your photograph under each style to see which one suits you best!

2 Look at recent photographs of people in your family, and at any photographs of older members of your family, taken when they were young. What family likenesses can you see? Draw what you think your face will look like in twenty or thirty years' time.

4 Draw a self-portrait or choose a favourite photograph of yourself. Glue it on to a piece of stiff card, large enough to frame the picture. Decorate the frame in an unusual way, either by painting it with patterns or gluing on sequins, lace, wrapping paper, tiny beads or shells.

Index

Amenophis I, **6, 7, 30**
Ancient Egyptians, **6, 8, 9, 30**

background, **8, 9, 17, 21, 27**
bronze, **22**
Byzantines, **11**

cameras, **27, 28**
canvas, **15**
cartoons, **31**
clay, **25**
crayons, **20, 29**
Cubism, **30**

drawings, **5, 16, 20, 28, 31**

felt-tip pens, **21, 29**
frame, **31**

Giacometti, Alberto, **22, 23, 30**
Greeks, **11**

Hockney, David, **26, 27, 30**

Maar, Dora, **18, 19**
magazines, **9, 25, 28, 29**
montage, **28, 29**
mosaic, **10, 11, 12, 13, 30**
mummy, Egyptian, **6, 9**

oil paints, **30**
outline, **9, 11, 20, 21**

Neptune, **10**

painting, **5, 14, 15, 16, 17, 23, 30**
papier mâché, **24, 25**
pastels, **8**

pattern, **8, 13, 18, 19, 20, 21**
photographs, **5, 16, 26, 27, 28, 31**
photo-montage, **26, 28, 30**
Picasso, Pablo, **18, 19, 20, 21, 30**
postcards, **31**
poster paint, **9, 16**
printing, **13**
profile, **5, 8, 20**

Romans, **11, 30**

sculptures, **5, 22, 23, 24, 25, 30**
self-portrait, **5, 15, 16, 31**
Singer Sargent, John, **4**
sketch, **12, 16, 20, 24**
studio, **27**
Surrealists, **23**
symbols, **6, 7**

texture, **16, 18, 19, 20, 21**
tin foil, **24, 25**
tombs, **6, 30**

Van Gogh, Vincent, **14, 15, 16, 30**

watercolours, **9**
wax crayons, **21**
wire, **24, 25**

Acknowledgments

The publishers are grateful to the following institutions and individuals for permission to reproduce the illustrations on the pages mentioned.
The Museum of Modern Art, New York/Bridgeman Art Library, London: cover; Musée Condé, Chantilly, Giraudon/ Bridgeman Art Library, London: 4; © The British Museum: 6; The Ancient Art and Architecture Collection: 10; Musée d'Orsay/ Visual Arts Library: 14; The Metropolitan Museum of Art, Jacques and Natasha Gelman collection, New York © DACS 1996: 18; Courtesy of Association Alberto and Annette Giacometti, Paris. Photo by Sabine Weiss, Paris, © DACS 1996; Tate Gallery, London: 22; David Hockney/Tradhart Ltd: 26.